Passive Income:

10 Unique Methods to Making Money Online and Achieving Financial Freedom

Table of Contents

Introduction

It's one thing to build a business. It's another to get married to it. Whether you have a day job or not, it's always a good idea to look for business opportunities that enable you to set things up and pretty much step away. I am, of course, talking about passive income systems that enable you to build your system once and earn money many times over without breaking your back.

Let's face it. If you wanted to bust a sweat, break your back, or otherwise put in a hard day's work, you have your day job for that. People looking for passive income want to maximize their rewards while minimizing effort. Keep in mind that building such systems require some capital. In the "real" brick and mortar world, this requires quite a bit of capital. After all, if you want to make money off residual income rights to songs or other intellectual property, you probably would have to pony up a pretty penny to get those rights in the first place.

Not so with online income systems. While you still have to spend some capital, it's a tiny fraction of what you would have to spend if you were to build an offline passive income system. Another example of this is real estate. Regardless of where you live in the United States or Western Europe, buying real property often involves bank loans and requires an extensive sum of cash. Whether you are renting out apartments or you are developing malls, this type of passive income can burn a hole through your pocket.

Thankfully, online passive income systems don't involve such financial drama. For as little as 100 hundred dollars, you can set up a viable online business. In fact, ViralNova, a blog that sold for north of a million dollars, was started on a shoestring budget. We're talking about less than a hundred bucks. If they can do it, you can do it too. If you're looking to build a nice passive income through the internet, you have come to the right place.

The Online Passive Income Strategy You Need to Learn

Now that I've gotten you excited about the idea of starting your own online passive income system, I need to step you back a little bit. Please understand that most of these systems would produce a trickle of income if you just set them up and let them run. That's right. If you were to just implement them and do the bare minimum in pumping up traffic or otherwise building them up, they would produce a trickle of income.

Don't get depressed just yet. Please understand that since these are very easy to set up and require very little cash up front, you can build many of them. Accordingly, to succeed with online passive income systems, you need to build as many of these businesses as possible. They produce small streams of income individually. But if you add all these up, it can amount to quite an impressive income river.

The next question you need to ask yourself is what are you going to do with that extra money? The answer should be obvious. You should then reinvest a large portion of that cash into even more assets. If you keep repeating this process, you can build such an extensive network of passive income assets that you can comfortably quit your day job and put relatively little work into your network of online businesses. You are then free to do what you want to do. In other words, you achieve financial freedom. And the best part to all of this is you don't have to be a rocket scientist or some sort of brain surgeon. This doesn't take genius-level skills. You just need to build up the system one site at a time.

Just like with real estate, if assets become mature, in other words, they start generating a lot of money, there is an existing market of buyers who would be glad to pay you top dollar to buy these mature assets. You have two possible income streams here: the actual income you generate from your websites as well as their sale value.

The key here is to understand that you are building assets that go up in value over time based on their performance. Once you have set up a nice online passive income network, your next step should be to diversify by buying offline passive income assets like rental properties or IP rights. Again, this can take the form of apartment units for rent, malls, commercial property, or song and book rights. The possibilities are endless, and the best part is you can start small with very little money. With all that out of the way, let's jump in.

Chapter 1: Republishing Viral Social Media Content

Have you ever checked out your Facebook timeline and noticed funny or shocking videos with a lot of likes and shares? Those are viral pieces of content. They go viral because there is a tremendous amount of online interest in that piece of content. What if you were able to piggyback on the viral appeal of such content to get eyeballs of people who would then click on your ads? The more they click, the more income you make, either on the front end or the back end if they buy something. Sounds awesome? Well, here's how you do it.

Step #1: Focus on a high-value niche

This is crucial. If you're going to be building a blog based on viral social media content, you must make sure that you are publishing a blog in the right content category. This must be a content category that advertisers pay top dollar for. Content niches are not created equal. You can post all the amazing high-traffic music videos you want but you'd have to settle for the pennies you get.

On the other hand, you can target foreign exchange, insurance or loans and get fewer eyeballs. However, when that target audience buy something, you are sure to get paid a lot more money. Focus on looking for content that fits high-value niches. How do you know if advertisers are willing to pay a lot of money for a niche? Naturally, this is very simple. You just need to go to Google Keyword Planner and pay attention to the cost per click of keywords related to the niche you're advertising. They should quickly let you know if there is enough advertisement or commercial value.

Step #2: Use software to quickly find and republish content on your blog

There are ready-made software applications that enable you to look for content based on keywords. Better yet, they can scrape such content and republish it to your blog. The key here is to republish the link with some screenshots. This way, the original rights owner still gets traffic and you are not technically stealing their content. Instead, you are just piggybacking on their content by having people click from your blog to go to the content that they like. This creates a win-win situation. The original rights and content owner gets traffic while you also enjoy traffic and possible ad clicks.

Step #3: Use software to reshare your blog content on social media and other distribution platforms

Using specialized software, you can then take the blog link that you created along with a nice-looking header photo designed to get eyeballs and share that material on social media, forums and other distribution platforms. The great thing about this is that the audience who already made that piece of content that you're resharing viral populates certain easy-to-find areas on Facebook and Twitter. You only need to reshare that content after you've repackaged it in those same areas. Don't be surprised if these people make your own version or repackaging viral. Sounds awesome, right.

Step #4: How to make money with this technique

To monetize this technique, you need to find niche-targeted affiliate ads. To get such ads, you need to join an affiliate program that targets your niche. You can go to places like Affiliate Vault, ClickBank, CJ, or PeerFly to find such ads. When your visitors click on these affiliate ads and they do something that the sponsor would pay for, maybe they would leave an email, or they would buy something, you earn a commission.

I suggest that you start with affiliate product ads first. Once you have mastered the art of increasing and optimizing your clickthroughs and conversions, you should step things up by going to the next level. The next step, of course, is to create your own products that are directly tied into the niche of your blog. Since you, yourself, created a product, your profit margin is close to 100%. The best part to this? You are in full control of how you advertise your product. You are also in full control of the quality of the product.

This increases the likelihood that you would be able to get the right product in front of the right eyeballs to maximize your conversions. The bottom line? More money for you.

Time commitment: Less than four hours per month

This technique only requires you to check the settings of your software to ensure that it's scraping the right content. Also, you need to make sure that when you reshare such content that you set them up properly, so you don't get banned on the places you're distributing your materials on.

Chapter 2: eBay Arbitrage

Arbitrage is a fancy word for buying from location A at a low price going to location B and selling that item for a higher price. Sounds familiar? It should. This is the classic case of making a profit by buying low and selling high. In this method, you're going to be buying cheaper items at Amazon and reselling them on eBay.

Step #1: Find product niches on eBay that sell at a higher price than Amazon

You need to spend a lot of time on eBay. Look through all their product categories. Zero in on products that are constantly sold. I'm not talking about stuff that is sold on auction every once in a while. I'm talking about stuff that is sold by a store using a buy-it-now button. This should give you a clear picture of products that are constantly on sale at a price that is higher than Amazon.

You probably would have to spend quite a bit of time on eBay to find such niches but let me tell you, the time you invested is more than worth it because if you find the right niche, you can pretty much lock in on an autopilot income system.

Step #2: Set up eBay listings for your products

Now that you have identified product niches that sell higher on eBay than on Amazon, the next step is for you to determine if it's worth selling. You only have two considerations here. First, the product must be selling at a decent enough market. Anything north of 12 to 15% is good. Anything below and it's kind of a dicey proposition.

Second, and this is just as equally crucial, there must be enough demand for the product on eBay. In other words, a lot of people have the product on their watchlist or there are other indications of consistent demand. You don't want to buy a product that is seasonal or has a limited audience that taps out easily. Put simply, you don't want to put up a product and after a few sales, it dies and then you wait a couple of months then it picks up again. Instead, you want something that sells pretty much evenly throughout the year.

Again, this requires quite an investment of research time. The workaround to this is you can hire a virtual assistant from places like the Philippines, India, Pakistan, Bangladesh, or any other country that has a large population of people who speak English as a second language. These individuals can do the digital legwork you need to do to ensure you are selling the right items that would enable you to earn a year-long income from eBay.

Step #3: Order products from Amazon when you get a sale

Now that you have set up your eBay storefront, you must wait for orders. If you use the right keywords and you set up your store properly, you shouldn't have to wait long. Once an order does come in, you need to turn around and order that product from Amazon. In the beginning, you probably would be stuck doing this manually.

However, once your store picks up quite a bit of sales volume, I would suggest that you automate this by hiring a programmer of Upwork to create a custom script for you. This system should automate you buying materials that were ordered from your eBay store on Amazon. Your profit? Is the difference. Obviously, it's the difference between the price you charge on eBay minus your costs and the price of the product you bought from Amazon.

How to Make Even More Money

You can set up this system, so you can make even more money by collecting client emails. You may want to add an extra step in the product fulfillment process that requires your buyers to enter their email into your notification system. Maybe you can give them some sort of digital freebie to incentivize them to sign up. Whatever you need to do, do it so you can create a nice list of tried and proven buyers.

Once your list fills up, create your own AliExpress Oberlo-powered Shopify store. This is a dropship store where your visitors can see your online catalog and then they click it to order. They order directly from a shop in China. The Chinese supplier, in turn, ships the product directly to them. You don't have to warehouse these products. You don't have to handle any product at all. You just make the difference between the price paid by your customer and the money you pay your suppliers.

If you have a nice mailing list from your eBay activities and you set up a Shopify store that caters to the same niche as your eBay store, you can stand to make quite a bit of money. This would be like shooting fish in a barrel because you would be selling to people who already have a track record of buying the type of niche products you have on your Shopify store.

Time commitment: Less than four hours per week

Chapter 3: Amazon Arbitrage

Amazon has this system called Fulfillment by Amazon. Essentially, you rent warehouse space from Amazon to store your products. When people buy those products from your Amazon store, Amazon does the backend fulfillment for you. They charge a tiny fee, and everybody is happy.

Theoretically, it creates a triple win. Amazon wins because it's able to offer more products on its website, thanks to its third-party stores. You win because you get to make a profit. The customer wins because they get faster delivery and more professional handling because the whole fulfillment process is handled by Amazon.

To make money off this system, you can either create a new product which you then sell on Amazon or you simply buy a product that already has a hot demand on Amazon from a supplier that charges a low enough price for you to make a profit.

The problem with the first option is that it's anybody's guess what the next hot product would be. It's not unusual for a lot of third-party Amazon merchants to lose money because they made the wrong bets as far as customer trends and tastes are concerned. In this method, we're going to focus on the second option: finding low-cost products and selling them at a profit on Amazon's FBA system. Here are the steps.

Step #1: Find high-dollar or moderately-priced niches on Amazon

The first thing that you need to do is to look for niches on Amazon that have a high volume of consumer interest. These are niches that sell all day every day. Next, make sure that the products that they move are moderately-priced or high-priced. In other words, you cannot focus on 1 to 10-dollar items. Your profit margin on such items is just so razor-thin that even if you have a high volume, whatever profit you make is probably not going to be worth the effort.

Shoot for something that is in the 40 to 100-dollar or more range. What's important here is to pair high consumer interest and sales volume with a high enough price. You probably would need to camp out in Amazon for quite some time or buy specialized software to find this information. Regardless of what you do, you need to do proper research because if you mess this up, you probably are not going to make any money with this method.

Step #2: Find wholesalers or direct importers online or in your area

Now that you have a clear idea of what you're going to be selling, the next step is for you to find wholesalers or direct importers of these products. These are already in the business of either manufacturing or distributing or both your particular target product. It would be a good idea if you can find them in your area or if you can find them online. If you have enough capital, you might import these directly from China.

Step #3: Use FBA to sell products a decent margin

The next step is to use the Amazon FBA system along with your Amazon store to sell these products at a competitive price. By this point, you've already done research on your competitors. You know how much they're selling these products for. You've also already cut deals with suppliers that give you a decent enough margin. What margin should you shoot for? Insist on 15% or better. If you can't get 15%, this is simply not worth doing.

Step #4: Sell using your Amazon store

The next step is to just push sales using your Amazon store. You must set it up properly with the right keywords and you must experiment with the content of your page until you get maximum clickthrough and conversions.

How to Make Money with This System

As you can probably imagine, this system is so simple and so accessible that a lot of people are doing it. In fact, many people are complaining that their profit margins are razor-thin. Still, I recommend doing this. How do you get a competitive advantage? Very simple. You offer bundles using low-cost value boosters. In other words, you take a group of products that have low margins and you throw in several low-cost products to inflate the perceived value of the bundle.

When you do this, you can charge a higher price for the low-cost value booster. You really don't have much room to move as far as the "anchor" products or core products in your bundle. However, since you're adding in one or a few low-cost items to boost the value, even if you were to make only a few percentage profits off the main products, you would still be able to command a big enough premium for the whole bundle, thanks to your value booster that you would come out ahead. Bundling remains one of the most powerful ways to protect your profit margin with Amazon arbitrage.

Time commitment: Less than 4 hours per week after you've set up the system

Chapter 4: Professional Paid Directory

There are certain professional services that cost a lot of money. For example, if you needed plastic surgery, you can bet that your cosmetic surgeon would probably charge a pretty penny. There are many niche services that cost quite a bit of cash. However, the people offering these services often don't have enough clients. They're always on the lookout for more paying customers. This is where you come in.

By creating a professional services directory and charging money for the promotion of it, you can get a lot of takers. In fact, as your directory gets more established and attracts more traffic, you can charge a premium because the cost per customer of these high-value services are quite high.

For example, each realtor's sale in California amounts to 6% of the sold property's value. If the value of the house is 3 million, that's a sweet 180,000-dollar commission. Realtors value their prospective clients this way. Accordingly, since they possibly stand to make that much, they would be more willing to spend more money in promotions and getting their clients. Here's how you set up this type of online business.

Step #1: Find high-value professions

The first you need to take is to find professions that charge a lot of money to end users. As much as possible, stay away from professionals that typically deal with subsidized payment systems. I am referring to Medicare and HMO. For the most part, doctors are out except for cosmetic surgeons. If you're stumped when researching these professionals, hire a virtual assistant to do the research legwork for you.

Step #2: Populate your directory initially through LinkedIn contact harvesting

When was the last time you ate at an empty restaurant? I would venture to guess that it has probably been a long time. When people see an empty restaurant, they psychologically link that detail to the quality of the food. At some level or other, they assume that since nobody is eating at the restaurant that the restaurant's food must be no good.

This creates a serious chicken-or-egg problem for any business. You need existing business to attract new business, but you can't attract new business because you don't have an existing business. Do you see the problem here? The same applies to your directory. You have to populate it, so you can start attracting paid or discount listings.

The best and easiest way to do this is to go through LinkedIn and do searches for professionals that specialize in the services you're going to advertise with your directory. As you can probably imagine, this takes quite a bit of elbow grease. A good shortcut to this is to simply hire a virtual assistant to go through LinkedIn using the target keyword search terms you give your assistant.

Step #3: Get traffic through social media highlighting content supplied by professionals you list

Now that you have populated your directory, your intermediary step should be to contact these professionals and ask them if they would like free "enhanced listings." An enhanced listing makes their business listing more prominent. When people visit your site, they would first see certain businesses listed front and center. This can get a lot of clicks and this can possibly lead to more appointments and clients for those businesses.

Once you have gotten professionals LinkedIn information, contact them and ask them if they would like this enhanced listing for free. You know, and I know that it's not actually absolutely and totally free. There's a catch. The catch is the professional must give you some content that's related to their service. That's their "entrance fee." Of course, you're going to feature this content on your site with the link to the source.

The real value of this content involves traffic. You're going to use this content that you did not generate to get traffic from social media. In other words, you win twice over by contacting professionals on LinkedIn to get listings and once you get them listed, a certain proportion of them would want to give you content which you, in turn, use to draw traffic from places like Facebook, Twitter, Instagram and other social media platforms.

The key here is to use this system to create a self-sustaining and self-propagating content and traffic generation setup. Eventually, it becomes easier and easier to get new listings because professionals could see that your directory is growing by leaps and bounds. Also, as time goes by, your traffic performance increases as more and more of your content become visible on search engines.

How Do You Make Money with This System?

To monetize this setup, wait until you get enough organic traffic from social media platforms as well as search engines. Once you get a decent and consistent traffic volume, contact people who are already listed on your site and ask them for premium page placements on the first page. Alternatively, you can ask them if they would like to buy advertising that's rotated to the site.

At this point, you're offering a very compelling value proposition because you are getting targeted traffic and consumers who go to your site are obviously already looking for service professionals. The benefit that you bring to the table is obvious. This increases the likelihood of you getting premium advertising customers.

Don't be shy about charging upwards of 5,000 dollars per month for top tier placement and visibility on your site. In fact, well-managed online professional services directories make hundreds of thousands of dollars a year due to a multitiered advertising offering. They offer first-page placement, banners, rotating links, and a wide range of other ad options.

Time commitment: Less than 8 hours per month

Chapter 5: Resell Fiverr Services

Fiverr is a huge online platform where people offering digital services (services that can be done remotely and delivered online) can sell directly to interested buyers. Originally, services were offered at five dollars, now five dollars is strictly optional. Despite its name, Fiverr offers ads from a wide range of freelancers starting north of that price. It's not uncommon to see Fiverr ads for certain specialized types of services starting at 100 dollars.

Be that as it may, Fiverr is a great place to find relatively low-cost specialized digital services. By buying these services at a low price and then reselling them at another website at a much higher price, you can stand to make quite a decent profit. Here's how you do it.

Quick note: This cannot be used for graphics services. You cannot use this technique when you are reselling graphics services from Fiverr. Fiverr puts a watermark on all its graphics drafts. Your customer can see that you are just reselling Fiverr graphics. Accordingly, you can't use this technique for reselling such services.

Step #1: Compile a massive list of online classified websites

Your first step is to find places on the internet where you can advertise Fiverr services at a much higher price. This can take the form of online classified sites, blogs that feature free ads. You can also advertise in the classified sections of forums. There are many websites that have at least one part of their digital real estate dedicated to people buying and selling products or services. Look for those websites. Create a massive list of them. Again, if you're having a tough time researching this material, you can hire a virtual assistant to do it for you.

Step #2: Find the most popular non-graphics services on Fiverr

The next step is to find services that are in heavy demand on Fiverr. Why? Well, the fact that they're in heavy demand on Fiverr means that there is a heavy demand online, in general, for that type of service. Search in terms of categories. For example, when you look for a logo designer, that's a category. Look at how many star reviews each provider has. If you notice that, on average, they get a lot of reviews, this means that there's a heavy enough order volume. Look for these service niches. Come up with a nice list of them.

Step #3: Offer such services on online classified sites using a central email address

Now that you have identified services that are very popular on Fiverr (which don't involve graphics), the next step is for you to come up with an ad advertising such services on the classified sites you've found with Step #1. The secret here is to make sure that all your ads use the same email address. This way, you make it easier on yourself. When people are interested in the service you're advertising, they only need to use that email address, so you can manage your whole service arbitrage enterprise using one email account. This makes it so much simpler.

Step #4: Use Mobirise for professional-looking mobile-friendly service site design

Mobirise is a great sales page design tool that doesn't require any coding skills. Anybody can use their drag-and-drop interface to create high-quality mobile device-ready webpages. Use Mobirise because it's quick and easy to create your own service site. It has enough icons, so your service site would look very professional. Put together a service site that advertises the Fiverr service category you are reselling. Buy your domain and put up your webpage on that domain. Take the URL of your service page and send it to people who email you looking for services.

Step #5: Tighten up your terms of service and implement a tight order fulfillment system

Here's the secret to making sure that you make money reselling Fiverr services. Please understand that the more time you spend bouncing emails back and forth with clients for this method, the less money you make. Your time is gold. Don't waste it clarifying misunderstandings with clients because you failed to properly explain terms in the first place.

Do yourself a big favor and figure out all the things that could possibly go wrong and create a term of service that clients need to sign up for before they could order your service. This minimizes the chances that they would keep coming back for a revision. Accordingly, most of your sales would take less time to process.

Ideal time commitment: Less than 20 hours per month

Chapter 6: Resell Software-Powered Services on Fiverr

There are many marketing software packages out there that truly deliver free traffic. Whether you're talking about getting traffic from Facebook, Twitter, or Instagram, there is no shortage of highly effective software that enables online publishers to get the traffic they need to make an online income.

As you can well imagine, there is quite a bit of demand for the output of such software. A lot of entrepreneurs may not have the time, energy or motivation to learn these software packages inside and out. Not surprisingly, they would be open to people offering output produced by such software.

Whether we're talking about social media traffic or search engine traffic made possible by SEO, there is quite a ready market for certain marketing output. With this method, you're going to buy such software and offer your output as a service on Fiverr.

You would take the specific details of your clients and feed it into the software that you bought. You then send your clients a report spelling out what you did and what they should expect in terms of traffic. Pretty straightforward.

The key here is to use such software to produce results in very little time. This is crucial. You cannot do this manually on Fiverr. You will be losing money hand over fist. You must use highly effective, integrated, and quick software to produce very fast results.

Step #1: Find traffic or SEO-boosting software on affiliate marketing sites

There are a wide range of affiliate marketing sites and there are always software packages on sale at such sites. These third-party software packages are a dime a dozen. Just make sure that you look at the reviews to ensure you buy a package that works.

Step #2: Offer the output of such software on Fiverr

Look at the traffic services section on Fiverr and see if you have any direct competitors. If you don't and you are sure that you can produce solid results with your software, post up and ad. Make sure you price your services correctly.

What I mean by this is you need to make sure that you get maximum value for time you spend producing that report for your client. It's not unusual for people to charge $50 per hour. You must convert this based on the actual output you are selling. How much time did it take for you to produce that output?

For example, if your target income is $50 per hour and you can produce results along with a report in less than 15 minutes, you should charge $12.50 or $15 for your report.

Step #3: Make sure it only takes you a few minutes to use the software and get output

This is the most important part of this method. If you are going to be using software that involves a tremendous amount of configuration, you will lose money with this method. It's like you're working a full-time job. The whole point here is to work as little as possible while making the most money.

The way you can do that is to pick software that enables you to produce impressive reports as well as results in as little time possible. There are software packages out there, especially for SEO and social media publishing.

Step #4: Scale up using a virtual assistant

In the beginning, you should perform this method personally. But as you get more and more clients from Fiverr and affiliate marketing forums, you should hire a dedicated virtual assistant from places like India, Pakistan, the Philippines, Kenya or any other country that has a massive population who speaks English as a second language.

In a lot of these places, $20 per hour is a very nice wage. Accordingly, you can hire a VA and contract with that person for a few hours of production every week. You can then resell the value of that person's output and charge a premium.

If you do this right, you would be able to employ a lot of virtual assistants on a full-time basis and making a tremendous amount of cash. Of course, this all depends on how well you recruit your clients.

Time Commitment: If you hit 40 hours per week, that is your signal to hire a virtual assistant. The whole point here is to work as little as possible while making as much money as possible. Thankfully, a virtual assistant would be able to help you do just that.

Chapter 7: Buy and Revive Dropped Domains with Solid SEO Value

What if I told you that a lot of websites that get a lot of traffic go belly up? For a wide variety of reasons, these websites are no longer maintained. They remain in a zombie or non-updating state until their domain registration runs out. Technically speaking, they drop out of the internet.

Do you see the opportunity here? You must remember that these websites used to get a lot of traffic. There are a lot of other websites linking to them. People are still clicking through. Unfortunately, they now see a "404" or "Page not found" error.

What if I told you that these dropped domains are gold mines? Seriously. You can make money from these websites through direct traffic or SEO.

Search engines look at link relationships between websites in determining how high to rank a site for a specific set of key words. If it turns out that certain domains get a lot of links and they rank high for certain keywords, it usually means that when these websites link to other sites, in turn, those other websites enjoy a boost in their rankings. Do you see the golden opportunity here?

Well, you're not alone because a lot of people are actively buying dropped domains with good SEO fundamentals and bringing them back from the dead. They would then set up very simple looking websites in place of those old sites.

When you look through the content of these resurrected sites, you can see that they link to other websites. That's their sole purpose. They just harness all these backlinks and pump them to target sites.

If done properly, those target sites enjoy a nice rise in their search engine results. They rank higher. Now, do you see why there's a tremendous demand for people offering a service where they buy and revive dropped domains and link to the websites of their clients? Best of all, you can make money on this on a recurring basis.

I've personally seen link packages charging $500 every month. The seller has a very nice network of high quality resurrected domain websites. If you buy his link package, you only need to pay $500 a month to get a nice boost for your own website's search engine traffic.

Imagine the long-term income of people who offer such services. We're talking big money here because such services usually sell out. It's not unusual for such websites to link to 2 different third-party sites, provided their dropped domain websites have enough pages. There's a tremendous amount of opportunity here.

Step #1: Use dead link checker tools to find niche-targeted dead domains

If you are going to try to make money with this method, it is crucial that you find niche-specific dead domains. You can't just take a dead domain and link it to an unrelated website.

For example, you can't resurrect a football-themed domain and link it to a website that sells kid's shoes. It doesn't make any sense. Google will probably penalize you. Therefore, it's crucial that you find niche-targeted dead domains.

There are many tools out there that would enable you to find such dead websites. One powerful free tool is Screamingfrog. It's a dead link checker, but it spits out a list of dead domains. You can then take these domain names and plug it into a bulk domain checker to make sure that they are truly dead.

Step #2: Use SEO forensics tools on your dead domain list

Once Screamingfrog or whatever tool you're using spits out a nice long list of dead domains and you have filtered them against the bulk domain checkers of domain registrars like GoDaddy or NameSilo, the next step is to use another set of tools to determine the SEO value or fundamentals of those dead domains.

Personally, I use Majestic and Ahrefs.com. These tools let me know how many backlinks a domain has and other very important indicators of SEO value. Most importantly, these tools will tell me which other pages linked to this domain.

If I notice that the domain gets a lot of gambling, pharmaceutical or porno backlinks, chances are, it's a spam domain. I don't buy such domains because they've been spammed to death and if I link to my client's website from that domain, they might get penalized.

Step #3: Buy dead domains

Now that you have thoroughly filtered your dead domain list to ensure that it's truly dead, is niche-related and has solid SEO fundamentals, the next step is to buy these domains using any old registrar.

Step #4: Install Wordpress

This is self-explanatory. You're going to revive the domain by installing Wordpress.

Step #5: Link to your target site for quick link juice

In other words, you're going to advertise that you're offering this service. Once you find a buyer, you then link from your revived blog, which you've filled with content to your client's target sites.

It's important to note here that you should charge monthly. You're essentially charging rent for your link. If they don't renew the rent, you pull their links. You stop linking to them. I've seen providers make tens of thousands of dollars every single month providing this type of service.

Time Commitment: Less than 8 hours per month.

Chapter 8: Buy and Revive Dropped Domains to Get More Traffic for Your Own Website

In the previous method, stepped you through the process of buying and reviving dropped domains, so you can start your own service business. The whole idea is to buy and revive dropped domains, and then sell links. These links go to your clients' websites.

If you do it right, they get a nice boost in search engine rankings, and they continue to pay "rent" to you month after month. This can translate to several thousand dollars of recurring income every month. That's right. You don't have to lift a finger. They send money through PayPal or bank wire month after month like clockwork.

Again, the whole point of this book is to help you build online businesses that require very little maintenance work. Once you have set them up, they start producing money.

The key here is to set these assets up once and work very little afterwards while collecting cash. When it comes to passive income, this is the name of the game.

For this method, you're going to through the same steps as Method 7 with one change. Instead of selling, the links to clients or promoting others' websites or pages by linking to them, you're going to set up your own website.

Maybe want to set up a blog and make money when people click on ads. Maybe you want to sell an online store with a blog. When people go in through the content pages, or click through to the product pages, and they like what they see, they then click a "buy now button". You make money through your drop ship e-commerce store. They're just so many ways you can skin this cat. The key here is to link to your own websites.

It's important to note, however, that your websites must share the same niche as your revived domain network. Otherwise, if there is such a far distance between your domain relevance and the niche of your website, you probably won't get as much traffic. Even if you did, these people possibly would not be interested in what you are promoting. Make sure you do this in a very niche-targeted way, or else you probably won't make much money out of it.

Time commitment: Less than 8 hours per month

Chapter 9: Find Low-Cost Designers on Marketing Forums and Enter Contests

What if I told you that there are contest websites on the Internet that pay at least $200 per contest? In fact, I've seen contests with payouts upwards of $1,000. That's some serious money.

The best part of all of this is you just need to enter a submission, and the contest promoter usually would give feedback. This way, you can keep tightening up and revising your work entry until you win the contest. Usually, the most persistent contest participants end up walking away with the prize.

Too many graphics designers would just submit an entry. If the contest promoter criticizes, or in any way give a critique, the contest participants would get turned off. They would not revise their work. Usually, there are a couple of people who keep revising until the contest promoter is happy. These are the individuals who win such contests.

If you want to make money doing service arbitrage where you buy somebody services for a low price, and you make more money out of it by winning contests, this is the opportunity for you. You just need to buy services from low-cost designers, and then enter contests that have a huge payoff. We're talking about 50 to 1, or even 100 to 1 payoff.

For example, if you come across somebody who is willing to produce a logo for $5, look to enter a contest where you can win upwards of $500. That way, your time, effort and attention to detail would be more than compensated.

Step 1: Find a pool of low-cost designers

Thankfully, there is no shortage of low-cost designers. You can find them on Facebook groups, Facebook pages, online communities such as forums, or even mailing lists like Yahoo groups. They're all over the place.

These designers, mind you, do not produce cheap work. They produce high-quality materials, but since they live in developing countries, they tend to charge a lower rate. It's not uncommon to find top-notch design work from India for the grand sum of $5.

It's important, however, that you do not obsess about price. What's the point of retaining somebody who charges a dollar for his work, but the quality sucks?

You need to ask for a free trial. They should design a custom banner or header for you. If you are happy with the design, you then put them on your list. These are people that you're going to contact if you join a contest. You may have to spend some time finding a long list of such high quality, yet low-cost designers.

Step 2: Enter contests with a value of $200 or more

Make sure that you enter contests at places like 99designs and similar websites that are valued at least $200. Anything lower, you're just wasting your time. It's not worth your time and attention.

Step 3: Use rejected entries for your own arbitrage design service website

Unfortunately, if you join a contest, you're not guaranteed to win. Nobody is. Even if you're the most persistent person there, if the contest promoter somehow thinks your design or skills are not good enough, you're not going to win that contest. What do you do in this situation?

You're probably out $5 to $10, as well as the value of your time. How do you recoup your investment? It's quite simple. Since the contest promoter rejected your entries, you can put that rejected work into your own service website. You can put together a portfolio. This way, when online publishers or entrepreneurs see your website and are impressed by your portfolio, they can order your custom-designed services.

Again, in this situation, you are doing arbitrage. You are buying from your designer at a low price, $5 to $20, and you are selling to online entrepreneurs looking for these specialized graphics materials at the rate of $200 to even $500. It's important to keep the margin high because you're going to be spending your time looking for clients, as well as looking for contests to enter. If you do this right, you would have a nice design agency business that requires very little of your time while producing a very nice profit margin.

Time commitment: Less than 40 hours per month

Chapter 10: Create a Passive E-Mail PLR Empire with Outsourced Texts

PLR or Private Label Rights is content sold to online publishers, giving them the right to republish, rewrite, or create derivative works based on such content.

You must understand that if you are an online publisher, and you focus on a very particular very or complicated niche, you probably don't have direct personal experience of such information. You may not be specialized enough to do a good job; therefore, you hire a writer who does. The problem is such specialized writers do not come cheap. This is especially true if your niche has something to do with insurance, legal services, medicine, you name it.

The more specialized the body of knowledge, the more you're going to pay for experts to write content in those niches. Therefore, online publishers have historically flocked to PLR providers.

These PLR entrepreneurs, for example, would hire for a lawyer to produce content that explains complicated legal issues to lay people. Instead of that lawyer charging you $300 per hour to write such content, you can buy that PLR package for a hundred bucks.

Instead of being out of pocket thousands of dollars, you get nice stack of content for only a hundred bucks. This sounds like an awesome situation, but not quite.

Siding with the release of Google Panda, simply republishing duplicate content from PLR sources is not going to help your website get more traffic from search engines. Therefore, for all intents and purposes, PLR website content is pretty much dead in the water. Then why am I talking about PLR? "Where's the opportunity?" you may ask.

Keep in mind that, when you send e-mail, it's not published on the web. It's a private form of communication. The only person that sees that content is the person you sent it to. Accordingly, such content is not penalized by Google Panda. It's not public information or publicly posted anywhere, so how can it get penalized by Google Panda?

Most importantly, it's e-mail content. In this realm, PLR is alive and well. It's seriously doing better than ever. There's a tremendous amount of money to be made with e-mail PLR.

How do you play this game? It's quite simple. You focus on hot email list niches. These are niches that a large chunk of e-mail marketers focuses on. I am of course talking about weight loss, meditation, self-improvement, certain types of personal finance, specific types of specialized medical information, and others.

The key here is to get high-quality, expert-written materials in those niches, and then sell those packages repeatedly to many different people. They save a lot of money because they don't have to hire expert writers. You make a lot of money because after you have paid you outsourced writer, everything else is profit. You can get an e-mail PLR package done once for $100, and make thousands of dollars over the life of that package.

Step 1: Find hot e-mail list niches

The first thing you need to do is to find very popular niches for e-mail marketers. To get this information, you need to go hang out at affiliate marketing forums.

People, based on their behavior, as well as their statements, would pretty much spell out what which niches are hot and dead cold. The key here is to look for niches that are hot in terms of turnover volume and popularity, while at the same time, commanding a high commercial value.

How do you know? It's quite simple. Look for keywords related to that niche and pop them into Google Keyword Planner for AdWords. You can quickly see if advertisers pay top dollar for ad placement that targets certain keywords related to the niche you're researching.

Step 2: Find talented Filipino or Indian writers

There are talented writers who speak English as a second language. These are college graduates. A lot of them have many years of experience. Additionally, a lot of them charge very little money. We're talking as little as 10% of what an American or Western European writer would charge.

Don't get too excited if a person just has great English writing skills. This is not enough. They have to be knowledgeable enough about those specific hot niches you are targeting. If they're clueless, then it's going to show in the materials they produce. Nobody's going to pay for those PRL packages because they're worthless.

You're really walking two tightropes here. On the one hand, you're trying to save a lot of money, so you're outsourcing to the other side of the planet. On the other hand, you must filter these writers to make sure they have specific knowledge.

Therefore, a lot of the legal information or legal assistance content is out sourced from the Philippines. There are a lot of Filipino lawyers who speak and write English well, and they are also familiar with US law. They then produce high-quality legal assistance materials at a fraction of US costs.

Step 3: Create lines of e-mail autoresponder sequences

It's important to understand that when e-mail list marketers do their thing, they're not just sending people one e-mail after another, they segment their communications based on where the recipients are in the buying process. Accordingly, you should create specialized lines of e-mail autoresponder sequences. These are automated online courses delivered over e-mail that give your list members the information that they're looking for.

It's crucial that you have a clear idea of the many different lines of e-mails your target market would want. For example, if I am a weight loss list marketer, I would know that there are different audience segments in my target market. Some people are just simply looking to stay toned. They've already lost the weight, and they just want to maintain their ideal weight. They require a different list of autoresponder messages.

Another segment involves currently overweight people who want to lose weight. They just want to shed the pounds. They don't care how. They just want results. These people require a different autoresponder sequence.

Finally, there are people who are very specific regarding how they should lose weight. Maybe they want to lose weight through a vegetarian diet. Others may prefer a ketogenic, high-fat, low-carbs diet. Even others might prefer a high-protein diet.

Whatever the case may be, you must create specialized lines of e-mail autoresponder sequences. Otherwise, your customers will not get the results they're looking for. They can run those sequences, but if those messages hit the wrong people and produce the wrong effects, they're not going to make any money. It's just not going to happen.

Step 4: Create once, sell many times over

The great thing about hiring outsourced writers to produce a large stack of e-mail autoresponder sequences covering a wide number of lines is the fact that you offer specialized e-mail content. You only need to create these once, and then you can sell specific parts of your library database for a tremendous amount of money.

It's not uncommon to charge $60 to $100 for an autoresponder sequence. Of course, the more specialized the sequence, the higher the price you can charge them.

Still, if you spent, let's say, $500 on a Filipino lawyer or an Indian insurance executive to write specialized content, you only need to sell that product a few times for you to get your money back. Everything else is gravy. Everything else is pure profit.

For example, you spent $500 for a lawyer from overseas to produce five lines of e-mail sequences, with each e-mail sequence costing $100 to online publishers. Accordingly, you only need to sell the package five times for you to start earning profit. What if you continue to sell those lines ten years from now? Do you see the profit potential? By that time, you would have created many other lines, and other customers would be buying those lines. This can add up to a tremendous amount of cash.

Make no mistake about it PLR, as a business model is no joke. It can make quite a bit of money. I'm just talking about selling the PLR package itself. You can also make money through upsells.

Step 5: Upsell your e-mail list

When an online entrepreneur buys an e-mail PLR package from you, a lot of the times, they are assuming that they would have to set everything up, and they would use that content to send to their e-mail list.

Often, a complete amateur would buy your stuff. They're just trying to get their feet wet in online marketing. They really don't know what they're doing, but they know they can save a lot of money buying your e-mail PLR packages. Those are your ideal customers because when they buy your content, you can follow up with related services.

You can tell them that you can set up their e-mail collection page. You can even input the content of the e-mail packages into their autoresponder software. Finally, if they are clueless regarding where to get traffic, you can supply the traffic as well.

Keep in mind that you're not going to be doing these directly. Instead, you are just going to be reselling a freelancer's service. For example, on Fiverr and other websites, there is no shortage of squeeze page or e-mail lists set-up specialists. You retain them for ten bucks, and you sell their service for $100 or $200 to your upsell clients.

Similarly, it's not unusual to find somebody from the Philippines, who charges $20 an hour a day for data entry. You then take that person's service, and repackage it as a $100-e-mail data entry package. You get the payment from your client, turn around and send payment to the Filipino freelancer. They e-mail autoresponder data to where it needs to go, and the customer is happy.

Finally, you can also resell traffic. There is a wide range of people offering traffic, and unfortunately, most of them are not good. Let's just get that the way; most of the traffic doesn't convert because if it did, those people won't be selling that traffic.

Your job in this situation is to filter decent traffic from regular traffic, which is quite lousy. Once you find decent traffic providers, you then upsell such traffic services to your customers. Don't be surprised if you can get away with 5 to 1, or even 10 to 1 markup. People are starving for decent quality traffic.

Time commitment: If you do this right, you would be able to do all of the above for less than 8 hours per month.

Conclusion

Keep the 10 methods above in mind if you are looking to set up a quick and easy passive income system on the Internet. Please understand that the name of the game is to set up as many of these systems on a regular basis. Each website may not make much money, maybe $20 to $30 each per month. You may be thinking that it's chump change, but if you were to make 100 or several hundred of these small, simple websites, all that money can add up. In fact, a lot of entrepreneurs set up such systems and automate them, so they work very little every month, while making several times their former job's full-time income.

Making money is a mindset. If you see the opportunity, money will appear. If your attitude is everything must be hand fed to you, or things are just simply impossible, regardless of how obvious the opportunity is, you'll never see it. It will just go over your head and pass you by. Which type of person are you? Start acting accordingly.

I wish you nothing but the greatest online business success.

I Need Your Help...

I wanted to thank you sincerely for downloading this book!

I hope this book was able to help you to start your journey to building passive income streams for your life and create a brighter future. I know the beginning will always be the toughest obstacle to overcome, but with determination and the right attitude, I truly believe everyone can achieve their dreams.

Some of the methods may seem a bit unorthodox to many, but they do work – if you are willing to work as well. These strategies were never meant to be a "get rich quick" tactics, but they will offer you passive income when done properly.

The next step is to take action and believe in yourself, you can do this!

Finally, if you enjoyed this book, then I'd like to ask you for a favor, would you be kind enough to leave an honest review for this book on Amazon? It'd be greatly appreciated! I take reviews seriously and will continue to improve them to best serve you.

Thank you and good luck!